MEMORY TRAINING
Improve Your Memory to Reach Its Unlimited Potential

By Basil Foster

By Basil Foster

FREE DOWNLOAD

INSIGHTFUL GROWTH STRATEGIES FOR YOUR PERSONAL AND PROFESSIONAL SUCCESS!

My friends and colleagues Joshua Moore and Helen Glasgow provided their best seller on personal and professional growth strategies as a gift for my readers.
Sign up here to get a free copy of the Growth Mindset book and more:
www.frenchnumber.net/growth

TABLE OF CONTENTS

Introduction 5
Memory Quiz 9
Long-term Procedural Memory Training 15
The Process of Mental Rehearsal 15
Movement Is Memorable 18
Kinesthetic Learning 18
Cueing Procedural Memory with Gestures And/Or Objects 19
What To Do When You Lose Your Place And How to Avoid "Action Slips" 20

Long-term Declarative (Semantic) Memory Training 23
Cognitively Active Study Technique Best Practices 25
Specific Learning Exercises That Access And Utilize Semantic Memory 26
Using the SQ3R Method Of Study 32
Creating And Implementing Semantic Long-term Memory Scripts 33

Long-term Declarative (Episodic) Memory Training 35
Putting Long-term Memory All Together 39
The Loci Technique 39

Short-term and/or Working Memory Training 41

Photographic Memory Training 45
The Memory Palace 46
The Memory Peg 50
The Military Method 51
Developing Your Photographic Memory Using A Deck Of Cards 52
Patterned Study Arrangements 53

- Visualization and Association Technique........ 54
- Mind Mapping 55

Mnemonics.. 57
- Body Part Mnemonics....................................... 58
- Musical Mnemonics 60
- Name Mnemonics.. 62
- Expression Or Word Mnemonics 63
- Model Mnemonics... 64
- Ode Mnemonics 64
- Note Organization Mnemonics 65
- Connection Mnemonics....................................... 68
- Spelling Mnemonics 70

Brain Games 72
- Brain Games For Short-term and Working Memory 72
- Brain Games for Long-term Memory................. 76
- Memory Games For Family And Friends.......... 77

Brain Workouts.. 80
- Take Up A Memory Boosting Activity................ 84
- Develop A Memory Exercise Routine 85
- Waging The War Against Distraction 87

The Health And Wellness Components Of Memory.. 91
Training 91
Memory Training Outcomes 102

Introduction

"Memory is the mother of all wisdom" – so said Aeschylus, the ancient Greek playwright and soldier. How incredible is it that each and every human being born before and/or since Aeschylus enters life with the potential for this built in wisdom? When viewed in these terms, it seems almost an obligation that we nurture, improve and preserve our memory to the best of our abilities throughout our lives. I've chosen to write this book as an exhaustive collection of memory training methods, techniques, exercises and tips, devoted solely to this worthy obligation. The benefits of training the brain to utilize the different types of memory available to us as human beings are measurable, numerous, and invaluable. Regardless of age, formal education, IQ or life experience, we are all capable of accessing the powerful "memory intelligence" within us and through the process of brain training exercises, improving the accuracy, speed of retrieval as well as the sheer amount of knowledge we can store within our minds.

Here are just a sampling of the benefits you will experience from memory training:

- Improved name/face recognition and retrieval: avoid the awkwardness and embarrassment of failing to put a name to the face of acquaintances or new business associates.

- Remembering birthdays, anniversaries and special days: the ability to remember not only the important days of a friend or loved one's life, but developing a talent for easily remembering appointments, business meetings and details of events that will impress people regardless of how long you've known them or how close you are, personally or professionally, to them.
- Never losing anything again: being able to locate keys, glasses, important papers and treasured mementos each and every time, because you've developed a fail-safe method of remembering where you placed objects that resonates specifically with the unique way your brain works.
- Having phone numbers, credit card numbers, PINs, account names and passwords readily accessible: remembering important codes, numbers and names without the security risk of writing them down and/or storing them where others could access them.
- Remembering how and when to take medication: alleviating the worry and danger of missing important dosages, whether it is for you or a loved one.
- Increased retention: extending the length of time you remember information you've read and studied for from hours or a

couple of days at best, to the rest of your life!
- Increased social ease: developing the talent to remember and tell entertaining jokes and stories.
- Prescriptively protecting the future of your memory: ensuring that your memories and ability to remember are preserved throughout your entire life.
- Free up "brain space" for new information: when you "just know" essential facts, you gain space for new knowledge and skills!
- Alleviate stress and anxiety: when your memory skills improve and your brain is firing on all of its cylinders, the stress and anxiety from "trying to remember" will disappear.

The next chapter of this book includes a short Memory Quiz that will help you determine what parts of your memory you may need to focus more attention to in order to assure that every element of your memory intelligence is in optimal working order. Your results will determine whether you need to strengthen your long-term or short-term memory abilities, as well as explaining what exactly these memory types are responsible for.

This book will catalogue specific exercises for the improvement of each and every element of long and short-term memory. I've also included chapters that focus on photographic memory techniques, mnemonics, and word association techniques, as well as challenging brain workouts and games to further hone and tone your memory!

If, as you read this book, you find that you wish you had the additional ability to read and comprehend the information within it at a faster rate, I also encourage you to purchase and read my last book, **Speed Reading: Read Fast, Faster**. The ability to read at the speed of lightning is a wonderful complement to memory training and when you put the two of them together you will end up with a dynamic duo of self-improvement superpowers!

Memory Training

Memory Quiz

Please answer the following questions, choosing the answer that describes your memory challenges most accurately.

1. My morning routine would go so much smoother if I could only remember:
    A. To consistently accomplish ALL the steps I need to follow, i.e., brush teeth, walk dog, feed cat, etc.
    B. Where I left my car keys, backpack, lunch bag, etc.
    C. What the newest code to my home security system is, that I just downloaded from my computer because I already forgot the one they gave me yesterday!

2. At work, I tend to waste the most time trying to remember:
    A. How to get into the latest version of the computer programs I need in order to perform my job.
    B. Phone numbers, names of work contacts, email addresses, etc.
    C. The last thing someone told me to do. This gets worse when I'm trying to multitask or if I'm under pressure.

3. My worst nightmare when hosting a party is:
    A. Remembering how to coordinate the timing of all the food, so I don't forget

something in the oven or leave something in the freezer too long.
  B. Giving someone who is lost directions on how to get to my home over the phone.
  C. Remembering the names of people's spouses, children and significant others minutes after I was introduced.

4. My worst nightmare when attending a party is:
  A. Using an unfamiliar appliance or convenience like a toilet, or an automatic ice machine, panicking, and not being able to figure out how it works, or worse, how to make it stop!
  B. Forgetting the punchlines of jokes, or losing my train of thought in the middle of telling a story or making a speech.
  C. Remembering the names of spouses, children and significant others minutes after I was introduced.

5. No matter how hard I try, I'm no good at:
  A. Remembering step by step directions
  B. Remembering simple facts like names of things or phone numbers
  C. Keeping information in my head for any length of time

6. The thing I hate the most about modern technology is:
  A. Memorizing procedures

Memory Training

   B. Memorizing account names and passwords
   C. Transferring temporary information from an email or text to another application, like filling out an application or gaining access to a website.

7. I wish I was better at:
   A. Remembering how to do things.
   B. Remembering facts and figures.
   C. Remembering short lists of things I need to do in the moment.

8. It troubles me when I can't remember:
   A. Directions to places I've been to before.
   B. The names of people I work with.
   C. Something important that I was told twenty minutes ago.

9. I annoy my friends and family when I can't remember:
   A. How to use the features on my smartphone or any new technology.
   B. Their phone numbers, birthdays or how old they are.
   C. Something they asked me to do a half an hour ago that I forgot.

10. Because I'm forgetful when it comes to certain things, I avoid:
    A. Giving any sort of directions or teaching others how to do things.

11

B. Using the internet, social media, online buying or anything that requires remembering passwords, codes or number sequences.
C. Going out of my routine or changing plans at the last minute.

11. When performing a task, I'm most likely to forget:
    A. How to do it in the proper sequence.
    B. The facts needed to perform the facts such as calculations, ingredients, or measurements.
    C. Verbal directions that involve more than two or three steps.

12. When I study for any kind of test, I have problems:
    A. Remembering processes and procedures.
    B. Remembering facts and figures.
    C. Remembering anything for any length of time!

The purpose of this quiz is to allow you to focus on the type of memory improvement you may be in need of, but please don't be alarmed if you wanted to circle several answers to one question! The fast-paced, stressful world we all inhabit these days can challenge the most mindful among us, and needing a bit of help and/or guidance when it comes to remembering everything we need to be is becoming a more and more common desire.

If your answers tended to be "A" responses, you need to improve your procedural long-term memory skills. Procedural long-term memory allows us to remember how to do things, from the most basic and automatic, including walking and talking, to more complex procedures, such as driving, playing sports or a musical instrument. We also depend on our procedural memories when performing any task that involves following multiple steps in a certain order, such as cooking or performing mathematical calculations.

If your answers tended to be "B" responses, you need to hone your declarative long-term memory skills. Declarative long-term memory allows us to remember and access facts and figures. Because we can store this "need to know" information, it also allows us to potentially free up memory space for new information. This information includes things like addresses, dates, number sequences, codes and passwords as well as general knowledge, and makes use of personal information as well.

If your answers tended to be "C" responses, you need to sharpen your short-term memory skills. Short-term memory allows us to temporarily store up to seven pieces of information (with a factor of 2 more or less) at a time until we no longer need the information, or decide to transfer it to long-term memory. These skills provide us the flexibility to use information in real time as well as to decide if we need to keep this information around for future access or dispose of it once our immediate needs have been met.

Now that you have a more specific idea of what type of memory skills you need to improve upon, I encourage you to read, learn and utilize the many different memory and brain training exercises I have collected for this purpose. Remember, everyone is different. Implement the exercises and routines that resonate with you. It's always easier to remember procedures and facts when they are meaningful to you, your lifestyle and the family and friends you make and share your memories with!

Long-term Procedural Memory Training

The routines and exercises in this chapter have been chosen specifically to focus upon and improve long-term procedural memory capacity.

The Process of Mental Rehearsal

Mental rehearsal, also known as visualization is a proven technique used by athletes, dancers, musicians, and surgeons, the military and even astronauts of practicing the steps needed to successfully perform a task in your head. As such, it is a very effective way to improve long-term procedural memory skills. The benefits include preparing for the best and worst outcomes of any multistep process and can be applied to just about any daily life situation. In this way you can practice and solidify the process you desire to commit to memory as well as identifying any concerns you may have, figuring out what to do if something goes wrong and integrating the different steps of the process into a cohesive whole. Mental rehearsal can be used to commit the following types of processes into your procedural long-term memory:

- Planning for an event that requires time and action coordination
- Teaching, presenting or public speaking
- Cooking complex recipes and/or coordinating an entire menu

- Learning and/or improving a challenging physical activity or routine
- Perfecting a complicated multi-step process such as computer programming, any type of construction process, writing an instruction manual or performing an experiment or research project
- Self-improvement goals, including weight loss, physical fitness, personal and professional growth projects

The Steps of Mental Rehearsal:
- Find a quiet space where you won't be disturbed
- Have pen and paper available
- No phones or other distractions
- Breathe deeply and close your eyes if it helps you focus
- Mentally walk through each step of the process. When you hit a point that worries you, imagine all the ways it could go wrong. Take notes if you need additional visual reminders.
- Identify then "Fix" all the potential mistakes that could happen
- After you've mentally gone through the process once, review your mental and/or written "to do" list, and repeat the process, implementing any safeguards you

may have added to guarantee the success of the procedure

Successful implementation of mental rehearsal will ensure not only the commitment of each step of the process into your long-term procedural memory, but will give you a readily accessible contingency plan for any and all unplanned eventualities. When you mentally rehearse a process, you are only limited to the boundaries of your imagination! The more details you add, including your five senses, the variety of emotions you may experience, who you might be with and what your environment is like, the more visceral and vivid the process will become in your procedural long-term memory, and the easier it will be to automatically access the process whenever you need it!

Basically, what you're doing when you mentally rehearse is making both sides of your brain work by using mental muscle memory. If you want to make the experience even more visceral, you can add actual physical movement to your rehearsal, making hand gestures and body movements that represent how you will physically move throughout the process. This adds actual muscle memory to the process, adding another "hook" for your long-term procedural memory to latch on to.

By Basil Foster

Movement Is Memorable

Expanding upon the idea that adding physical movement enhances and improves long-term procedural memory skills, it is important to understand the automaticity of procedural long-term memory. Basically, the beauty, and the mystery of procedural long-term memory is that it is unconscious. Once we learn a physical process, such as riding a bicycle, the procedural section of our memory locks the process into place, and even if decades pass between bike rides, our bodies will automatically remember how to ride when the opportunity presents itself. Having this innate and seemingly limitless memory capacity, and not accessing it more seems almost criminal when viewed as a lost educational opportunity. It is no wonder, then that many educators have learned to incorporate physical movement into a spectrum of learning activities for all ages and abilities based upon the solid theory that accessing procedural long-term memory as an aid to memorizing subject matter, transfers that knowledge, through movement into our long-term memories. What a fantastic use of educational scaffolding and what an unbeatable argument for the inclusion of physical activity in educational settings!

Kinesthetic Learning

There are people who learn much more intuitively by doing rather than reading or studying. Through physical activity such as

dance, debating, role-playing or charades, they stimulate long-term procedural memory, which catalogs and stores this physical activity as an automatic process. If you know or think you might be a kinesthetic learner, it is most important that you find physical activities that resonate with your learning style and access your long-term procedural memory capacity. Activities that promote and improve long-term procedural memory include:
- Improvisation and physical comedy
- Rhythm and rhyming based activities
- Painting, sculpting and model making
- Repetitive stories and games

Cueing Procedural Memory with Gestures And/Or Objects

Research conducted by the VA suggests that patients with healthy long-term procedural memory but who might be suffering from other forms of memory impairment were able to be cued by gestures that often accompany spoken words. These common, often universal hand movements, stimulate and access procedural memory, unlocking automatic action sequences.

Another promising cueing method, used for patients suffering from dementia or Alzheimer's disease, is using objects related to the action sequence that is trying to be accessed, such as placing an empty laundry basket in a room to cue washing or folding clothes or setting up a coffee center to cue making a pot of coffee.

So the next time you find yourself challenged by consistently following the steps of a process or procedure, try cueing yourself by watching videos of the process that include demonstrations and gestures, or remind yourself of the task by setting out a task related object, such as an empty garbage bag or the next mornings can of cat food.

The takeaway from these cuing methods, as well as the other techniques discussed in this chapter, is that procedural long-term memory can be accessed in many different ways. Therefore, if you want to improve your long-term procedural memory capacity and its efficiency, you should be aware and knowledgeable of all the intuitive as well as learned behaviors available that stimulate and motivate this powerful gift of the mind.

What To Do When You Lose Your Place And How to Avoid "Action Slips"

Have you ever been driving somewhere and all of a sudden you have no idea what to do next? As disconcerting as this may be, it is also quite common. Usually after a fleeting moment of complete panic, you shake your head, take a deep breath and as suddenly as you forgot, you go back into automatic mode and everything is rosy again. What happened? Like as not, some small detail like a road detour, or a new traffic light crept into your subconscious and the invading information collided with your procedural memory and made everything stop for the briefest moment. The best thing you can do when this happens is relax, recoup and save the reviewing process for a more appropriate time when you are not behind the wheel. On the polar opposite of the consciousness spectrum, a similar event called "choking" can occur when you are thinking way too much about an automatic process, to the point where you experience the worst form of self-sabotage and again, momentarily forget what normally is as instinctive as breathing. This overthinking can happen to athletes and performers when they are under enormous competitive pressure. The antidote for this situation is the same: relax and basically stop thinking!

There is a third instance when this loss of procedural memory can occur which is known as an "action slip". Action slips are a form of forgetfulness that are not really a memory glitch. Absentminded mistakes such as starting one task and completing another, or driving to one destination, and ending up in quite another often happen during highly automatized activities when we are preoccupied or distracted. Action slips may also include an intrusion of another automatic process that share a resemblance to the intended activity. If a routine has been altered in any way or the environment changes action slips are also more liable to happen. You can also lose your place, such as when you are in the middle of cooking a recipe or two activities can blend when you multitask or project what you need to do next; or you may even experience procedural reversal when you get confused between two steps of the same task. The one thing in common with all these examples and variations of action slips, is that they all happen during action sequences. The best thing you can do when an action slip occurs is to refocus and keep your mind on the task you are performing in the moment. You can also position objects that you are using, such as ingredients, on the other side of your task to signify you have used them. Multi-tasking or thinking ahead of yourself is the bane of automatic sequences, so try to be mindful when you are on automatic, as ironic as that may sound.

Long-term Declarative (Semantic) Memory Training

As we move into Long-term Declarative Memory Training, I have chosen to further deconstruct this type of Long-term Memory. This chapter will focus on exercises and routines for preserving and improving Semantic or general Declarative Memory and the next chapter will be devoted to Episodic or personal Declarative Memory.

Semantic Declarative Long-term Memory is responsible for our ability to learn and remember general knowledge, such as street names, the capitals of states and countries, historical timelines, mathematical formulas and vocabulary.

Here is a general guide to learning and retaining new information using Semantic Memory:

- After the initial exposure or lesson: spend a few minutes reviewing new data about 10 minutes after learning it. You should now be able to remember it for 24 hours.
- Review again the next day.
- Review again in one week.
- Review again in one month. This data should now be easily retrievable from your semantic long-term memory.

What is the difference between cognitively passive and cognitively active study behaviors?

Basically the difference between these two

methods of study is the level of and commitment to independent active participation. Depending upon how much time, effort and personal interpretation you are willing to invest, your success at learning and retaining information will directly reflect your total investment. Cognitively passive learners show up to class, listen and take notes. Cognitively active learners access and stimulate their semantic long-term memory capacity by:

- Asking how and why questions.
- Designing their own charts and graphs that represent the information they are learning in a visual manor that resonates with them.
- Breaking down complicated sequences into individual steps.
- Writing their own review questions.
- Reorganizing the information they have learned in different ways.
- Comparing and contrasting the information they've learned in order to gain a working knowledge of it.
- Looking at how all the facts fit into the bigger picture.
- Trying to figure out the answer based on the information they've learned, before looking up the answer.
- Finding connections between pieces of information.

- Drawing and labeling diagrams from memory instead of copying them over and over.

Cognitively Active Study Technique Best Practices

- **Practice Memory Retrieval**: Give yourself frequent self-tests by retrieving new information from your long-term memory and fact checking it for accuracy and attention to detail.
- **Teach It**: Try to teach someone else what you've learned in your own words with your own examples. Listen as they reflect back what you've taught for accuracy and attention to detail.
- **Acknowledge Your Weak Areas**: place extra focus on areas of knowledge that you have trouble retaining and/or retrieving from your semantic memory.
- **In Your Own Words**: Rewrite original notes, using your own words. If you are having trouble with a particular section, realize that you may not completely understand this particular element and work to deconstruct it until you do understand it. Think of challenging information as a big knot you need to thoroughly untie in order to get a straight through line of knowledge.

- **Don't "Cram" The Knowledge in—Immerse Yourself Over Time And Allow It To Sink In Gradually:** Spread periods of study over several days, rather than marathon study sessions. Always give yourself time to process information. Review frequently to expose weaknesses and give yourself more time to focus on understanding them completely.
- **Avoid Multitasking:** Multitasking is a focus disruptor and an attention distraction. It prohibits the memory from encoding information into easily accessible long-term semantic memory.
- **Review Before Bed:** Reviewing new information right before you sleep gives your brain a concentrated period of time for your semantic memory to accept and consolidate new material into long-term memory.

Specific Learning Exercises That Access And Utilize Semantic Memory

Maintenance Rehearsals and Elaborative Rehearsals

As we know from the last chapter, mentally rehearsing a process can be a very valuable and productive way to ensure that the process is encoded in the procedural long-term memory.

There are two other variations of mental rehearsals that help us when we are fact gathering for short and long-term memory purposes. Maintenance Rehearsals are the intense techniques we use to remember a small piece of information in order to complete a task. An example of maintenance rehearsing would be when someone repeats a phone number over and over until they can actually dial it on the telephone and make the call. The goal of this rehearsal is not permanence – it is merely to temporarily capture the phone number mentally until it can tangibly be dialed into the phone. The purpose of Elaborative rehearsal is to permanently encode a fact, figure or code into the Semantic Long-term Memory. As such, it is a much more detailed exercise than the single focused but ultimately disposable maintenance rehearsal.

- Steps Of An Elaborative Rehearsal
    o Think about the fact you are trying to remember
    o Try to connect the new fact to knowledge that you already have in your semantic long-term memory by...
    o Using various techniques to "hook" the new fact to related older facts you already know.
    o Result: You now understand the fact, rather than simply memorizing or "knowing" it. It's

the difference between learning to read and reading to learn!

Examples of Elaborative Rehearsal:
- Using the name Roy G. Biv to remember the colors and and sequence of the rainbow: red, orange, yellow, green, blue, indigo and violet
- You need to remember what the French word *degoutant* means: you realize that it has the same number of syllables as its English translation, disgusting, and they both start with the letter "d".
- You need to remember the piriformis muscle in order to treat sciatica as a massage therapist. You look up what it means (it is the rectangular back stabilizer muscle located in the gluteal region), find out what it does (helps stabilize balance for the entire posterior of the body), look at a diagram, see its exact location and think about how it relates to things you already know (the sciatic nerve runs through it; therefore if the piriformis muscle is tight, it will squeeze around the sciatic nerve and cause sciatica!). If you rehearse this sequence in your mind several times then you will understand the piriformis and

will be more likely to remember it. This is literally an example of "muscle memory!"

Semantic Priming

Semantic priming is another technique that will allow you to hook new knowledge to facts that are already stored in your long-term memory:

- Write down a new word or term that defines or closely relates to the fact you are trying to learn.
- Think and list all the words you already know that relate to the new word.
- Review the new word in the context of being a part of the group of words you listed.
- Result: You now have a relatable group of words that will enable you to remember the new word.

Example of Semantic Priming:

- The term I need to learn is sous vide, a type of French cooking where sealed bags of ingredients are cooked in a water bath.
- I write down the term sous vide.
- I then write down all the words I can think of that relate to the term sous vide:
    - French; cooking; boil; Ziploc bag; water; sealing; chef; caterer; moist; locked in; steamed; contained; vital; vitamins.

- Result: I now have a relatable, descriptive group of words that will help me remember and understand the term sous vide.

***Note: it's very important to understand that this group of words is only for you to remember the word or term. It doesn't need to make sense to anyone else. It is your personally resonant word group.

Using Retrieval Cues

Retrieval in learning terms is the process of accessing information from the long-term memory, where it has been stored for this purpose. The process of retrieval is stimulated by a cue which can be a question, experience or event that summons prior associated knowledge. Cues then are the vital key that unlocks this information. Only when we have the correct retrieval cues can we recover the necessary information to transform information to implementable knowledge.

Retrieval based learning is a relatively underused strategy for long-term retention, but it is remarkably effective as well as easily transferable from the classroom to the workplace.

How To Practice Retrieval:
- If you have access to practice tests or practice questions about the information you have learned and are trying to

retrieve, practice with them but don't look up any of the answers or use your notes.
- Make up your own questions – This can be a bit time consuming but you are actually already participating in the retrieval process simply by creating the questions.
- Get paper and pen and simply list everything you know about the information you are retrieving.
- Want a more creative outlet? Draw everything you know on the topic from memory
- Organize your ideas into a chart, diagram or map.

After you have practiced retrieval learning, check yourself using reliable sources to test how completely and accurately you retrieved the information. This last step affords you immediate feedback about what you know and don't know.

A few last retrieval learning tips:
- Remember –when you recall you also relearn!
- Self-checking at every stage of retention ensures accuracy and efficiency.
- Always use real life scenarios in your retrieval learning. Examples that are "ripped from the pages" of your own life story will always resonate better than made up examples.

- Share your retrieval results –Talk about and explain your retrieval learning with others. It will help you retain the information and you may gain a valuable insight from another person's perspective on the subject matter.

Using the SQ3R Method Of Study

In 1946, the American educator Francis P. Robinson wrote a book called *Effective Study* that included the SQ3R Method of Study:
- SURVEY the material you want to learn. Read it through it quickly. Focus on chapter titles and subheadings as well as the first sentence of each paragraph.
- QUESTION yourself. Ask yourself multi-part, interesting questions about what you just surveyed to help you mentally organize the material for your second reading.
- READ the text again. Read thoroughly and carefully this time, keeping the questions you came up with in the second step in mind. Don't highlight passages or take notes.
- RECITE what you just read. Recite it to yourself or to someone else. Appealing the words aloud will deepen your understanding of the material. When you are finished reciting aloud, take notes.

- REVIEW the text. Include your notes, and wait a day or two before you perform this step. Think about other information you may already know that relates to those new information. Review your questions from step two. Have you answered them all thoroughly? Do you have new questions? Review the text quickly a few more times over the next several days or weeks to help consolidation into the long-term memory.

Creating And Implementing Semantic Long-term Memory Scripts

We make up and use Semantic Memory Scripts to acclimate and prepare ourselves with a customized blueprint of how events should proceed in certain situations. An example of a Semantic Memory Script would be going to the movies: you buy tickets, purchase popcorn and soda, watch some previews, watch the feature film and leave during the credits. These scripts are created through repeated practice and eventually stored in the semantic long-term memory. Semantic scripts save us time, effort and ultimately memory capacity. If certain repetitive events in our lives are encoded in semantic scripts then we can automatically recall them when we plan and experience the scripted event, saving our mental and memory energy for new and/or different events. Semantic scripts enable us to experience automatic flow and ease instead of re-experiencing the first-time mechanics of the same type of event over and over. Semantic scripts also bridge the gap between fact gathering and personalizing factual information to meet and reflect our personal needs and desires, creating the episodic long-term memories that we will explore further in the next chapter. When Semantic and Episodic memory joins forces, truly innovative and creative memory forces are forged and the potential for memory preservation and improvement is potentially limitless!

Long-term Declarative (Episodic) Memory Training

I think it's safe to say that the inclusion of Episodic Long-term Memory in your memory toolbox is a necessary one. Things literally get personal when it comes to Episodic Memories. An Episodic Memory is autobiographical; it contains the who, what, when, where and why of knowledge, as well as the emotions associated with past personal experiences. Remembering your wedding day or what you wore on your first day of school are both examples of episodic memory. If Semantic Long-term Memory access and retrieval denotes the difference between knowing and understanding, Episodic Long-term Memory access and retrieval denotes the difference between knowing and remembering!

As I mentioned at the end of the last chapter, there are important connections between Semantic and Episodic Long-term Memory, and when the two join forces, the memories made and stored offer rich, textured vibrant knowledge sources that can be accessed and retrieved for understanding at every level.

Episodic Memory basically animates and personalizes the factual knowledge gathered by the Semantic Memory, because it supplies the remembrance of time, place, personal participation and observation as well as the ability to recall the exact emotion experienced during the event that has paired up with semantic facts, figures and codes. For instance, if we look at the word "cat" solely through the lens of semantic memory, we can list physical attributes, behaviors, food sources, etc., but when we add in episodic memory the word "cat" becomes fleshed out, and comes to life through our customized, individual experiences with this particular animal. I will always remember a wonderful story a friend of mine told me about her niece when she first encountered my friend's very expensive, very high wired Abyssinian Cat. Sometime later Sandra was passing the time with her niece by asking her what sounds different animals made. The cow mooed, the pig snorted, the doggie barked, but when she asked her what sound a cat made, her niece, arched her back and hissed with arrogance and rage! And that, dear reader, is the meeting of Semantic and Episodic Memory at its funniest and finest.

I believe when people worry about losing memory, nine times out of ten, they are talking about losing Episodic Memory. Episodic memory is a large part of who we become as well as an emotional map of the course of our entire lives. It's no wonder that many people start prescriptively working to preserve and improve their capacity for memory at a relatively young age.

If Episodic memory is a visceral "reminder" of what's truly important in our lives, it also demonstrates that often it isn't grandiose desires that fuel our search for improved memory performance and capacity, but the little daily abilities that memory both affords us, and, when not properly maintained, seems to rob us of. The following tips and tricks are focused on the daily tasks and events that make our life go smoothly when our memories are engaged, but fill us with frustration, embarrassment and a vague sense of dread when they aren't.

Learning and remembering new names:
- When you are introduced to a new person, physically STOP what you are doing, and take a moment to register what has just happened.
- Use the new name in the dialogue you are having with the new person, and keep referring to this name in conversations you continue to have throughout the day.
- Think about whether you like this name or not.
- Think of other people you know who share this name.
- Associate the name with an image. Ex.: Elizabeth – famous historical painting of Queen Elizabeth I (1533-1603). Alternatively, image of current Queen Elizabeth II wearing one of her fabulous hats.
- When you get home or have access, record the new name either in an address book, a journal or using an online calendar or app.

Remembering where stuff is:

- Have "homes" for things you regularly use and/or lose, like keys and glasses.
- Say the name of the item out loud when you put it away somewhere.
- When you put an object down, make a point of looking down at it after it is in place.

Remembering what people tell you:
- When someone tells you something important, ask them to repeat what they said.
- Ask the person to repeat it slowly, so you remember how they said it.
- Repeat what you have just been told to yourself.
- Record the important statement on your cell phone or add it to an online calendar that will alert you periodically of the statement.

Remembering stuff you need to do:
- Write yourself a note and place it somewhere you will see it, like your door or your kitchen table or your bathroom mirror.
- Enlist a relative or friend to remind you of the task.
- Give yourself a visual cue by leaving out a task related object that you will see. Ex: gardening gloves to remind you to weed

or empty milk carton to remind you to go to the store.
- Set alarms on your cell phone that remind you of a task with the date and time you need to accomplish it by.

Putting Long-term Memory All Together

Before we move on to the next chapter and short-term and working memory, I would like to present an ancient Greek memory technique, used to this day, which allows you to access your procedural, semantic and episodic memory functions to remember a multipart speech or presentation.

The Loci Technique

- Picture a route you know very well, such as a walk you take with your dog or your commute to work.
- Take note of all the major landmarks, like stores and playgrounds along the way
- Now think of the major points of your speech or presentation and assign each point to one of the landmarks on your route.
- When you give the speech or presentation, think about the route and the various landmarks.

- The image of each landmark will remind you of the next major point in your speech or presentation.
- To reinforce each landmark with its assigned speech/presentation point, imagine something about the assigned point happening at its coordinating landmark. Ex: the point you are emphasizing is that you are in favor of pets in assisted living facilities. The landmark you have assigned this point to is the ice-cream stand on Smith Street. Imagine an elderly lady sharing an ice-cream cone with a collie at the ice-cream stand and you will easily remember the point you are trying to make!

Short-term and/or Working Memory Training

We've now come to the chapter where we will focus on short-term and/or working memory. I like to think of short-term memory as the clipboard, or temporary holding place of the memory system. Basically, short-term and/or working memory acts like the introductory hand shake with new material. Short-term memory finds itself time and time again in an information dating scenario: the attentive but discerning recipient of various bits and pieces of random facts, figures, images and language, but always working the room, in search of the next introduction that will be "the one." It is that vital piece of information worthy of being consolidated and encoded into long-term memory. For a long time, it was generally accepted that a person could hold 7 pieces of information, plus or minus 2 items, at one time in their short-term memory. Recently that figure has been adjusted down to 4 items, which is ironically inconvenient, considering the current demands of our fast-paced society.

Unless your future plans include studying neurology, it will suffice to consider the term "working memory" to be interchangeable with short-term memory for the purposes of this book. If you want to know the basic, but subtle difference between the two however, both function as temporary storage and clearing house facilities for information, but working memory can also organize and manipulate this information.

So what can you do to get your short-term or working memory in peak condition?

Let's start with some general tips and tricks:

- Don't multitask: Try and do one thing at a time. Otherwise your brain needs to make a choice and decide what item is more important than the other, when both items may have value.
- Avoid interruptions, interferences and distractions: Short-term memory is highly distractible. Don't tempt it to go off on a wild goose chase.
- Focus: Be in the moment. Forget about what happened yesterday or what might happen tomorrow.
- Verbalize your intent: If you need to learn a number or a name you need to remember, say it out loud.
- Bait your short memory trap: If there is a subject you need to learn for work or pleasure, memorize a few basic facts about it. This will act as memory bait, to attract bigger chunks of information about the subject into the trap we call memory.
- Record your thoughts: Old school writing is more effective than typing or keying in information and the concentration it requires helps you remember better.

- Enjoy nature: Taking a walk in a natural setting can improve short-term memory. Or look at a picture of a natural setting if you can't spare the time for a break in the woods.

Short-term memory has another function besides being the filter and clearing house for any and all information that enters our consciousness or unconsciousness. It also serves as the emergency center for information with a short but vital importance. Information that, in our ever more technology based society depends on the ability and availability of capturing codes, number sequences, temporary passwords and security cache combinations, and typing them in a specific area within a limited amount of time. The better you are at accessing and passing these code tests, the more you need to thank your short-term memory.

If you are not a natural at remembering number or letter sequences, there is a specific technique that will improve your accuracy:

How Chunking Works:
- Chunking is the action of breaking up information into smaller chunks
- You might not be able to remember the number sequence 5284693571, but if you break it up like this: 528 469 3571 your mind would probably recognize it as a phone number and you would remember

- it more easily because it has been chunked into a more recognizable sequence.
- You might have trouble remembering how to spell Mississippi, but if you chunk it up like this: MISS ISS IPP I your mind will respond to the separate syllables as well as to the implied rhythm of this chunked version, and you will very likely spell it successfully.

We have now covered the major types of long and short-term memory, how they work, what information they gather and how a piece of information is picked up by the short-term memory, filtered and, if deemed worthy, transferred to the long-term memory, where it is consolidated, encoded and stored for future access and implementation.

This book will be devoted to the comprehensive cataloguing of major memory enhancement, preservation and improvement techniques, exercises and routines, all of which have been developed for and proven successful at targeting the challenges of maintaining the peak performance and robust memory health that today's busy world demands.

Photographic Memory Training

The Oxford Dictionary defines photographic memory as "the ability to remember information or visual images in great detail." This realistic and accurate definition may vary from the urban myth that when someone has the power of photographic memory they merely need to blink their eyes to store an image of what they were looking at and keep it there through eternity. But there you have it. Photographic Memory does exist and is a powerful tool but it is just that –a tool, not a magic spell that transforms your brain into a digital camera!

There are people born into this world with rare memory "gifts" that many people confuse for photographic memory. Eidetic Memory and Superior Autobiographical Memory are the names of these rare conditions and you can't develop either of them. Eidetic Memory is the ability to visualize an image for a brief time after it's been removed. It is a rare condition that has been discovered in a very small number of children and even fewer adults. Superior Autobiographical Memory is an even rarer condition that enable individuals to remember almost every moment of their lives. It is debatable whether Superior Autobiographical Memory is truly a gift, as its recipients are endlessly bombarded by memories. If you give them a date, including the year, they will be able to recite exactly what happened to them from the time they woke up until the time they fell asleep.

There are several techniques you can enlist to develop the powers of a photographic memory. They include an ancient technique known as The Memory Palace, another variation called The Memory Peg, and a third one known as The Military Method. I will now give you instructions for all three:

The Memory Palace

The Memory Palace is an expanded version of the Loci method I explained in an earlier chapter, used to help remember major points in a speech or presentation.

Step One: Think of the layout of your house. This will be your Memory Palace. Your house is an ideal setting for the memory palace because you should be extremely familiar with every nook and cranny of it. The more little details you can visualize about your house, the sharper your photographic memory recall will eventually be.

Step Two: Pick your path. Once you have envisioned a detailed layout of your house, you will need to plan a path through it. For example, you might walk through the front door, into the sunken living room, then up the stairs into the kitchen. You might then go into the downstairs bathroom, then down the hallway to your home office. From the office you might climb the stairs to the upstairs family room then out the sliding doors onto the balcony. It is important that the path you choose is one you know very well and that when implementing The Memory Palace technique, that you follow the same exact path every time. Choose a definite starting and ending point. In my example this would be the front door and the upstairs balcony.

Step Three: Details, details, details... Close your eyes and imagine yourself at your starting point. (I will use the details of my example for clarity). I am at the front door. It is yellow and has a wreath of spring flowers on it. Now walk past your starting point into your Memory Palace. Look slowly from left to right. What can you see? I am in a small stone tiled foyer. As I sweep my eyes from left to right I can see a grandfather clock, stairs leading to the open living room, a fireplace, leather couch, trunk and rocking chair. There is a painting of my favorite cat over the mantle of the fireplace. It is important that you consistently observe and catalogue the details you are envisioning in an organized, defined manner. For example, always scan the area of the palace you are envisioning from left to right.

Continue walking through each room of your palace, following the path you have previously chosen and noting unique details as you pass through each area. Note: The more details you can visualize in your Memory Palace, the more items you will be able to memorize in the next step.

Step Four: Make the photographic memory connection. To sum things up to this point: you have determined that your home is your Memory Palace, you have determined the path you follow through it, and you have mentally followed this path, visualizing as many details in each area or room of your palace as you can. Now take each palace detail you have envisioned and connect it to something you want to memorize. For the purposes of this exercise let's use items I need to pack for a business trip.

I definitely need to pack your high blood pressure medicine! Make a connection between your starting point (my front door) and this medication. Here's where it gets fun! The more silly, unique or strange the connection is, the more likely you will be to remember it. Don't create a boring or general connection. The success of the connection depends on detail and information. I'm going to make a memorable connection between my front door and my blood pressure medication. First I place myself in my Memory Palace. Then, as I open my front door, I see a giant orange pill bottle blocking my entrance, bobbing back and forth like a child's punching bag toy. I can hear the sound of all the pills shaking around inside the bobbing bottle! Guess what I'm not going to forget to pack! It's that simple.

As you continue your trip on the path through your Memory Palace, you continue to connect items you need to pack in a memorable way to the details you've envisioned in every area and room of the palace. Don't fall into a theme however. If the giant pill bottle blocked your path through the front door and your next item to pack is toothpaste, don't have the toothpaste block your entrance to the stairs of the living room. Instead let the tube of toothpaste graciously lie down on the stairs, creating a ramp for you to slide down on!

Step Five: Time to tour your Palace! Once you have linked every item on your packing list to a detail in your Palace, you need to envision the entire circuit of connections from your starting point on the path to the place in your Palace that your list ends. When you are new to this technique you should make several tours, to ensure you have consolidated the entire list in a correct and accurate order to your long-term memory.

It will take time and practice to perfect The Memory Palace photographic memory technique but your ability to remember lists, sequences of events, timelines and systems will dramatically improve as you familiarize yourself with this method. You can use any location that is familiar to you, such as your college dorm, your parent's home or your cottage at the beach. Alternatively, as in the Loci exercise from the chapter on episodic memory, you can also use familiar routes such as your commute to work, walks or school runs, using landmarks instead of room details.

The only problem with using The Memory Palace technique is that no matter where on the path the piece of information you need to access is positioned, you will have to follow the entire path from starting point to ending point to reach it. This is an A to Z process, and individual items cannot be pulled out of it randomly. As you get better at the process, you can "fast forward" to the item you need, but you still have to go through the entire process until you reach the desired detail/item.

The Memory Peg

The process of Memory Pegging is similar to that of The Memory Palace, but instead of connecting information to details in a location, you link them to a list of numbered words called memory pegs.

Step one: Make a list numbered one to ten, of random single words.

- 1 = gum
- 2 = frog
- 3 = tulip
- 4 = candy
- 5 = sweatshirt
- 6 = tree
- 7 = box
- 8 = heart
- 9 = sock
- 10 = cat

Step two: Connect each numbered word to something you want to remember. Let's use my packing list as an example:

I need to pack my blood pressure medicine so I make the following link:

Blood pressure medication: Picture pills that you can chew like gum and when you blow bubbles your blood pressure goes down.

I need to pack toothpaste: Picture a frog brushing his teeth!

I need to pack my running shoes: Picture me running through a field of tulips
And so on and so forth...
So basically in order to use this photographic memory technique you need to link the items you need to remember to a list of memorized words, using memorable connections that inspire a vivid image. This technique works really well for lists of things you don't necessarily need to remember forever like grocery lists and packing lists. Save The Memory Palace for information you want to hang onto like processes and procedures you need for work, or important personal dates and data. This technique is flexible as you can incorporate as many random words as you need to fit your list of things to remember. There are actually lists of word pegs you can access on the internet if you get stuck coming up with random words.

The Military Method

I have included this method of photographic memory access, even though it seems a bit over the top, in its objective of enabling you to literally recall an image exactly as you first observed it. Although there are numerous articles and online posts touting the benefits of this method, there doesn't seem to be actual proof that this is really how the military trains their operatives to develop a photographic memory. Please also note that this technique will take at least a month to develop and must be practiced daily. Apparently missed days can set your progress back at least a week.

Step one: The environment. You will need a dark room (windowless bathroom is ideal), free from distraction. You will also need a bright lamp or ceiling light. Position yourself for easy access to the light source without having to stand up.

Step two: Prepare. You will need a piece of paper that you have cut a rectangular shape out of, the size of a normal length paragraph in a book. Have a book or other piece of writing that you are trying to memorize and cover it with the piece of paper, exposing only one paragraph. Make sure you are positioned so that your visual distance from the exposed copy allows you to focus on the words instantly when you open and close your eyes.

Step three: Practice. Without getting up, turn off the light and let your eyes adjust to the dark. Flip the light on for a second and then off again. Theoretically this action should give you a visual imprint of the exposed paragraph you were looking at. When you feel the imprint has faded, flip the light on and off again, while staring at the exposed paragraph. Repeat this process for 15 minutes every day for a month. If you are doing this consistently and correctly you should begin to develop the ability to scan and retain an image of the entire paragraph, word for word, in your memory.

Developing Your Photographic Memory Using A Deck Of Cards

Memory Training

Here is a memorization technique using a deck of cards to help you improve photographic memory.

Step one: take any deck of cards and memorize the face of the top three cards

Step two: shuffle the three memorized cards into the deck randomly spread out the shuffled deck.

Step three: pick out your three memorized cards. Put them in the order you picked them up from the top of the deck when you first chose them. Repeat this process every day for a week.

Step four: in week two pick up the first 5 cards from the top of the deck and repeat the steps of the process above for a week. Week three: 10; week four: 15; week five: 20; etc. Repeat stepped process, adding 5 cards a week until you can memorize faces and picked up positions of entire deck.

Patterned Study Arrangements

Here is an image-themed way to study notes or index cards.

Step one: write the main concept of what you are trying to learn on a note or card and position it on the center of your desk or work surface.

Step two: write related information on separate notes or cards and position them in a spider pattern around the centered concept note.

Step three: As you study, note the position of each note in relationship to the spider pattern.

Result: When you need to recall the concept and supporting information, you should be able to easily picture their positions in your mind's eye and access the photographic memory of it.

Visualization and Association Technique

This is a technique used often by various memory performers, based on the following three principles:
- Images are easier to remember than facts
- You have to focus when you create an image in your mind
- When you recall the image you reinforce the visualized material in your long-term memory.

How it works:
For the purpose of this exercise let's memorize the name of a triangle: Equilateral. An Equilateral triangle has 3 equal sides and three equal angles of 60 degrees each, adding up to 180 degrees.

Step one: convert the sound of the word to a mental image
- Equilateral: the sound of equal is a gift! The sound of the 3 remaining syllables "lat"; "er" and "al" remind me of 3 "equal" angles.

Step two: visualization: Because I know that each angle it the same and has to total up to 180 degrees, I can now envision the number 60 three times, forming an "equal" "angle" triangle.

Bonus: the words "equal angle" sound very similar to Equilateral!

Mind Mapping

Mind Maps were created in the 1960s by an English author and educational consultant named Peter "Tony" Buzan, who adapted this process from Leonardo da Vinci. When used instead of conventional lists, it stimulates the brain by structuring information more like the brain functions. Mind maps basically "map" out your thought processes using images, color and key words to stimulate ideas.

The benefits of mind mapping include:
- Adaptability – Can be used for lectures, note-taking, outlines or lesson plans.
- Flexibility – It's easy to add ideas at any point in the process
- Readability—allows relationships between thoughts, concepts and ideas so that facts are not disconnected
- Individuality—can be personally customized to resonate with individual preferences.
- Condensability—can streamline lots of information into a flowing creative process with a unified through line.

What you will need to Mind Map:
- Blank paper
- Colored pens and pencils
- Your brain and imagination

Step one: turn a blank piece of paper sideways and locate the center of the page.

Step two: Draw an image or a picture in the center of the page. This is your concept or central idea.

Step three: draw related images and write one word ideas around the central image. Use as many colors as you wish, as color adds vibrancy and excitement and stimulates the brain visually.

Step four: Connect the outer words and images to the central theme image with drawn, curved lines. Don't connect with straight lines. The brain considers them boring.

Result: You end up with a resonant, individualized, visual map of your thought process which you can not only refer to at a later point, but which, by its inherent visual and image themed nature is easily condensed and encoded into your long-term memory!

Photographic Memory Techniques run the gamut from practical to theoretical, but share a common understanding that memory loves imagery. As the classic saying goes, "A picture tells a thousand words" and those pictures can also access and hook into your memory mind with astounding results.

Mnemonics

A mnemonic (pronounced ne-mon-ic) device is any learning technique that helps access, consolidate, encode and retain information in the memory. Mnemonics use numerous encoding, retrieval and imagery tools to aid the access, consolidation, encoding, retention and retrieval of information to the memory mind. The primary objective of any mnemonic device is to make the association between information and the memory more meaningful, so that the memory will "hook" more easily on to it and thus allow the brain to experience better retention. The popularity and success of mnemonics down through the ages is based on the observation that our minds grasp and retain spatial, personally resonant or relevant, spontaneous or surprising, physical, sexual, funny or otherwise humanly relatable information rather than cut and dry facts and figures.

The word mnemonic is derived from an Ancient Greek word meaning "of memory, or relating to memory' and is related to Mnemosyne, meaning Remembrance, the goddess of memory in Greek mythology. Ancient Greeks and Romans believed there were two forms of memory: "natural" memory that is born within us and "artificial" memory which is learned through a variety of mnemonic devices. As I noted earlier, both the Loci technique and The Memory Palace photographic memory techniques were invented in ancient times. In fact, in order to remember historic dates, they would expand upon this idea of a house or a route, creating entire imaginary towns, divided into districts, each containing 10 houses, each with 10 rooms and each room with 100 potential memory landmarks, in order to encompass the four figures of the date desired to be remembered for all time!

There are many different types of mnemonics including mnemonics that incorporate parts of your body, music mnemonics, name mnemonics, expression or word mnemonics, model mnemonics, ode mnemonics, note organization mnemonics, connection mnemonics and spelling mnemonics.

Body Part Mnemonics

Knuckle /Valley Days In A Month:
- Clench your two fists and put them together. Beginning at the left most knuckle on your left hand, list the months starting with January. February falls in the first "valley" between the knuckles, March is the next "knuckle" month etc., until you reach the fourth knuckle of your right hand fist, which is December. All the knuckle months have 31 days! All the others (except February!) have 30.

Body Pegging System:

- Use the following parts of your body to create an impossible to lose or forget memory pegging system:
    - 1 = Fingers of right hand
    - 2 = Palm of right hand
    - 3 = Right Elbow
    - 4 = Right Shoulder
    - 5 = Head
    - 6 = Left Shoulder
    - 7 = Left Elbow
    - 8 = Palm of left hand
    - 9 = Fingers of left hand
    - 10 = Eyes
    - 11 = Nose
    - 12 = Mouth
    - 13 = Ears
    - 14 = Chest
    - 15 = Tummy
    - 16 = Behind
    - 17 = Right Knee
    - 18 = Left Knee
    - 19 = Right Foot
    - 20 = Left Foot

This kinesthetic and visceral pegging system was created by brainbox.co.uk and is a wonderful example of connecting a pegging system with familiar words that coordinate with a specific place on the body, which can then be associated with a list item and reinforced with an action that is specific to the body part! Ex: left foot = roll of paper towels. You could remember this association by kicking the paper towel roll with your left foot.

Musical Mnemonics

Probably the most famous music mnemonic would be "The Alphabet Song". Musical Mnemonics are responsible for much more than a popular children's learning song however. They are the backbone of an entire marketing industry! Radio and TV jingles are one of the most profound ways major corporations get our attention. How many times have you caught yourself singing along with a jingle, and like as not, without even thinking you know every single word? This is not just a happy coincidence for the business you are singing about. Music is a very powerful tool for making a lasting association between information and emotion and episodic memory.

Sing Your Way to Success

Step one: Take any list of items you need to remember for a test, a process at work or a party you are planning.

Step two: Put the list to a popular song you know the melody to. Sing it as you do other things like clean the house, pick up the kids from school or take your morning run.

Step three: Self-Check, especially in the beginning that your song lyrics haven't morphed from the original list. Although these alternative lyrics may be amusing, they won't help you when you need to take that test!

Result: If you do this for a couple of days, not only will this list of items be firmly positioned in your memory, but I dare say you may very well remember it years later! That is a statement of fact...and a warning!

Mnemonic Devices for Music
Alternatively, you can also use mnemonics to learn about music. The ultimate example of this would be the song, "Do Re Mi" from the musical The Sound of Music. Not only is the song a musical mnemonic but it's a song that teaches you the notes on the scale and associates them with related images! It really should be the theme song for mnemonics...

Memorizing Music Note Sharps and Flats
If you look at the keys on a piano, you will notice that there are black and white keys. The black keys are a half tone up or down from their adjacent white keys and are called sharps and flats. An easy way to remember the names of these keys in key signature order is this spoken mnemonic phrase:

- **F**ather **C**harles **G**oes **D**own **A**nd **E**nds **B**attle

The beginning letter of each word is the name of a sharp note in order: F#; C#; G#; D#; A#; E#; and B#

Simply revers the order for the names of all the flat notes in key signature order!

61

By Basil Foster

Name Mnemonics

I've already mentioned the most well-known name mnemonic: ROY G. BIV which represents the colors of the rainbow in order sequence. Another example of a name mnemonic is HOME which represents the names of the Great Lakes (Huron; Ontario; Michigan and Erie). You can easily create your own name mnemonics when you need to remember a group of related items. Simply take the first letters of each of the items and mix and match them until you come up with a memorable name.

EX: Types of vocal ranges: Base; Alto; Tenor and Soprano = BATS (for further associative reinforcement, visualize members of a choir flying around in black choir robes)

A Mnemonic To Remember Names And Faces

One of the most awkward social situations is when someone greets us by name but we can't remember for the life of us who they are! Here is a mnemonic designed to foil that very problem:

Step One: When you are introduced to someone notice the first feature on their face that stands out to you. Ex: Green Eyes

Step Two: Take note of their name. Ex: Mindy

Step Three: Make a memorable association between the two: Mindy sounds like Minty. Mint is Green like Mindy's eyes!

Extra Reinforcement: Every name has a stressed syllable. The name Mindy, for example has the stressed syllable Min in it. Within the stressed syllable there is usually a word; in this case the word is "in". Take the word in, which should remind you of Mindy and associate it back to Mindy's green eyes. Come up with a memorable statement. I look "in" her Minty green eyes: MINDY.

Expression Or Word Mnemonics

I already used an expression or word Mnemonic in the music section, with Father Jones Goes Down And Ends Battle, but perhaps a more well known example is: Please Excuse My Dear Aunt Sally, which stands for the order of operations in math (Parenthesis; Exponents; Multiply; Divide; Add and Subtract) It's very simple to make your own expression or word mnemonics. Simply:

Step one: Take a group of items you need to remember. Ex: The 5 largest cities in the U.S. - Chicago; Houston; Los Angeles; New York and Philadelphia.

Step two: Come up with a memorable expression that coordinates with each item's first letter: Ex: Cantaloupes Have Large Netted Peels.

It gets trickier when you also need to put a group of items into an ordered sequence: Ex: If I want to memorize the 5 largest cities in America from largest to smallest I would have to group them in this order: New York; Los Angeles; Chicago; Houston Philadelphia.

My revised memorable expression associating name and size order might be something like this: Never Leave Children Here Please! (Which works pretty well, because you wouldn't leave a child in a big city!)

By Basil Foster

Model Mnemonics

Model Mnemonics use supportive graphics and images to reinforce the concept or process that is trying to be remembered. My example of how to remember an equilateral triangle was an example of a model mnemonic when I encouraged the reader to envision three sets of the number 60 forming the equal angles of the triangle. Often the supportive graphics will literally illustrate what the words or figures are actively doing.

Another example would be a model mnemonic describing the parts of a story plotline. If line drawings supported the words describing the different parts, this would offer a memorable active visual cue. Ex: Exposition = flat line; Rising Action = ascending line; Climax = the pinnacle of two lines; Falling Action = descending line; and Denouement = another flat line.

Ode Mnemonics

Ode Mnemonics or rhyming mnemonics are similar to musical mnemonics where the association is reinforced and supported by words sung or spoken in rhythm and /or rhyme. A classic example of an ode mnemonic would be this ageless adage:

30 days hath September, April, June, and November.
All the rest have 31
Except February my dear son.

It has 28 and that is fine
But in Leap Year it has 29
Another example from my school years, although a bit more contemporary, is the following multiplication ode mnemonic:
I ate and I ate till I was sick on the floor.
Eight times eight is 64.
I can surely attest to the fact that this stuff sticks with you!

Note Organization Mnemonics

Note organization mnemonics are all supportive study systems, designed to reinforce information that has been learned and now must be retrieved for examinations, papers or oral presentations.

Note cards are useful to organize information in a way that resonates and is memorable to you. They can provide an excellent self-check device if you write possible test questions on one side and the correct answers on the other. You will then be able to test yourself or others as many times as you feel necessary in order to be prepared for written and/or oral examinations. Note: It is always preferable, once you are confident of your knowledge to write questions and answers in your own words, as the act of composing and writing reinforces the information/memory association.

Outlines are excellent, highly customizable knowledge "skeletons" upon which you can flesh out concepts and main points with details that are personally memorable. If you are unsure how to construct an outline, look at the image section online and view as many different types as you need to extract the elements that speak to your needs. Remember: when it comes to outlines, less is more. You only want enough written description to remind you of your main ideas and concepts. Too much information will inhibit your memory mind from working from inside the boundaries set by a solid outline.

The Cornell System of notetaking was created in the 1950s by Walter Pauk, an education professor at Cornell University. It entails dividing the note taking paper into several sections, dedicated to specific goals of the note taking task. Main ideas or questions are written on the left hand sign of the line and details or answers are written on the right hand side of the line. This system offers a clearly delineated visual cue between concept and detail, as well as enquiry and answers. Here are the details:

Preparation
Step one: draw a horizontal line across the bottom of your paper, about 2 inches from the bottom edge. This section will be dedicated to summarize your notes.
Step two: draw a vertical line down the left section of your paper, about two and a half inches from the left edge of the paper. This section will be dedicated for reviewing your notes.
Step 3: Leave the largest right hand section of the paper as your note taking area.

Taking Notes

Step one: write the course name/date/and lecture or reading topic at the top of the page.

Step two: Take your notes in the large right hand section. Include any information that the professor writes on the board or shows on a PowerPoint.

Step three: Use notes to listen or read actively. Listen for verbal/written cues marking important information. Ex: the three most important.... Also make note of any information that is repeated. These tips are for lectures as well as reading on your own.

Step four: Less is more. Focus on just getting key words and points down so you can keep with the lecture or understand what you are reading. Use bullet points, shortcuts, abbreviations as well as any personal note taking symbols you may have developed.

Step five: Record big ideas, not detailed examples. This will force you to make connections between the ideas presented and your own interpretation of them. This will enable you to remember the material later.

Step six: Leave a space, draw a line or start a new page when a new topic is introduced. This automatically organizes the material.

Step seven: Make a note of any questions you think of while you are listening or reading.

Step eight: Edit your notes sooner than later. If there are parts of your notes that are unclear or don't seem to make sense, fix them while the material is still fresh.

Reviewing and Adding Detail

Step one: Summarize key points. Pull out the main ideas or key facts from the right hand section. Write condensed versions in the left hand column. Use key words or short phrases that clarify the big idea or concept. Reviewing notes within a day or so of the lecture or reading really improves retention. If it resonates with you, underline or highlight key points. Also, cross out unimportant information. This system will teach you how to see the big picture and discard the unnecessary.

Step two: Write questions you think might be on exam in the left hand column. These will make a valuable study tool later on.

Step three: Summarize the main ideas in the bottom section of the page. Write this in your own words.

Using Your Notes to Study

Step one: Read your notes, concentrating on the left hand column and the summary at the bottom.

Step two: Use your notes to test your retention. Cover the right side of the page. Quiz yourself by answering the potential questions you wrote down in the left hand column. Now uncover the right hand side and check your answers for accuracy.

Step 3: Review notes as often as possible. Don't cram. Spread studying over a longer period of time.

Connection Mnemonics

Connection Mnemonics associate information that needs to be remembered with information that is already known. Here are a couple of great examples:

Mnemonic for remembering which way to turn screws, knobs, lightbulbs, etc.: Lefty loosey/ Righty tighty

I love this device because it associates directions that I understand with tightening and untightening which I seem to need to be reminded of. There is also a nice use of alliteration and rhyming, which always reinforce memorable associations.

Mnemonic for remembering which way Stalagmites and Stalactites grow:

StalaGmites: Grow from the Ground
StalaCtites: Come from the Ceiling

This device has so much going for it! It gives me direction, associating it with common letters in the word as well as the direction words. It gives me visual images to work with. Even the way the type in the words is set, gives me additional visual cues!

Connection mnemonics are often quite practical and deal with those day-to-day memory challenges that we can't quite get a grip on. Here are a few more:

How to remember the major roman numerals: (50, 100, 500, and 1000)

Lovely **C**adbury **D**airy **M**ilk: L=50; C=100; D=500; M=1000

Sequential (left to right) order of the Presidents on Mount Rushmore:

Washington, Jefferson, Roosevelt, Lincoln
Why **J**ust **R**emember **L**incoln?
For future reference, there are websites on the internet that list mnemonics by categories, so the next time you can't remember the exact order or directions or color of something, look up the mnemonic for it. Like as not, there will be one to fit your need!

Spelling Mnemonics

Spelling mnemonics can be used for specific difficult to spell words as well as for remembering spelling rules. Like connection mnemonics, they are very helpful practical and clever reminders that will help tricky spelling issues to be resolved and retained in our mind memory once and for all!

Here are some great ones:
- Never **believe** a lie.
- Emma faced a dilemma
- A new env**iron**ment will iron me out
- That liar looks fami**liar**
- An island **is land** surrounded by water.
- Rhythm **h**elps **y**our **t**wo **h**ips **m**ove

Here are some spelling rule/word meaning mnemonics:
- Use the word RAVEN to remember when to use "affect" vs "effect"
    - R emember
    - A ffect
    - V erb

        - E ffect
        - N oun
    - Complement/compliment
        - Compl**e**ment adds something to make it **e**nough; compl**i**ment puts you in the **lime**light
    - Sculpture/sculptor:
        - A sculPTURE is a kind of piCTURE

As we move on to brain games and workouts, I hope you have enjoyed learning all about mnemonics, how they can help our memory minds in almost any way you could ask for as well as how you can create your own personally memorable mnemonics to meet your specific memory challenges.

I leave you with this:

How do I remember how to spell mnemonics?

Use the first letter of each word: [There is no "M"—this spells NEMONICS] Now Erase Man's Oldest Nemesis, Insufficient Cerebral Storage!

Brain Games

Brain games include a spectrum of tests and exercises, games and teasers that stimulate how your brain functions, including your memory mind. Although brain games are currently trending, the thought process behind them as been around for hundreds of years. Putting together Jigsaw puzzles are a classic brain game that will help you work on your visual-perceptual skills which are vital when using visual cues to make memorable associations for memory consolidation, retention and retrieval. You can also time yourself when putting together a puzzle, which will hone your processing speed. Sudoku, solitaire and dominos are all popular brain games that involve sequencing skills, which, again are so important for procedural long-term memory tasks. Finally, crossword puzzles are a perennial favorite in the brain game circuit, involving and improving not only mental flexibility and sequencing, but adding a language component that can be beneficial for people who have word retrieval challenges.

The following brain games and exercises have all been chosen because they access memory function in one way or another. Good luck and have fun!

Brain Games For Short-term and Working Memory

- Say the numbers one through ten out loud. Now say them alphabetically...Start

Memory Training

with eight! See how fast you can get at this.
- Add up the numbers in your date of birth. Now add up the numbers of all your family's dates of birth. Ex: 2/4/62 = 68. Try to do all the math in your head!
- Name three objects for every letter in your first name. Try increasing the number of items per letter to make it more challenging. Ex: MARY = mittens, mold, money; ants, artichokes, Arizona; ring, roly-poly, raft; yellow, yacht, yes
- Look around the room you are reading these words in. In two minutes, find 5 green items that will fit in your pocket and 5 red items that won't. Switch colors and item numbers and decrease time for more of a challenge.
- Recite the alphabet backwards. Time yourself!
- Add up the numbers in your telephone number. Go to your contacts in your cell phone or address book, and see how many telephone numbers you can add up in five minutes.

Ex: 568 plus 379 plus 4126 = 5,063
- Make a list of 10 items and try to memorize it. Ten minutes later see how many items you can remember. Now try it in a half an hour. How about in an hour?

Next, alphabetize the list and see if it helps you remember the items! See if you can remember the items for a longer amount of times when you do this.
- Do math in your head while performing a physical activity, such as walking. Use birthdates again for a memorable source.
- Write down a five digit number. Look at it for 5 seconds. Turn the paper over and write down the number from memory. Now try this: Write down another 5 digit number. Pause and take a mental picture of the number, imagining focusing the camera on the number and hearing the snap as you take the picture. Turn the paper over and write down the number from memory. Try increasing the amount of digits to challenge yourself.
- Visualize the spelling of your street name in your head. Now try and think of other words that begin (or end) with the same two letters. Give yourself a time limit for more of a challenge.
- Take your grocery list and ask yourself WHY you are buying each of the items. Turn over the list and see how many items you can remember, using the why answers to help you.
- Now take your grocery list and make up a story about the items. Ex:

- Bag of lettuce
- Toothpaste
- One pound of sliced turkey
- Pack of double AA batteries

John ate a bag of lettuce and then needed some toothpaste to remove the pieces that got stuck in his teeth. His wife made a giant sandwich with one pound of turkey and put a new pack of double AA batteries into her camera so she could take a nice picture of it.

- Find an unfamiliar children's book and select an illustrated page. Look at it for 30 seconds. Close the book and write down everything you can think of from it. Now open the book up to the page and note every detail that you missed or forgot about. Pick a different page every day for a month and repeat this exercise. Look back through your descriptions at the end of the month and see how much you have improved.
- Play the suitcase game with family and friends. Take turns adding an item into an imaginary suitcase. The next person repeats the first item and adds another. This goes on and on repeating all the items in the correct order and adding another one until someone makes a mistake.

- Practice backwards spelling. Take any word and spell it backwards. Time yourself and see how much time it takes you to correctly spell 10 words backwards.

Brain Games for Long-term Memory

- Draw a map from memory. Think of a familiar route you travel and then draw it freehand. Compare results with a map and check how accurate you were.
- Play the teaching game. If you having difficulty learning a process or multiple step task, teach it to someone else. Have them stop you every time they don't understand something and don't move to the next step until you are both clear!
- Draw famous logos without looking at them. Compare your drawings with the actual logos and note where you misrepresented or omitted details.
- Think of a simple task like making a bed. Now think of all the different ways you could ask or teach someone else how to complete this task. You can words or actions. You can make up a song, a poem or a mnemonic. You can draw pictures, play a game or use symbols. Your imagination is your only boundary!

- Get paper and pencil and start listing all of the kids you can remember in each of the classes you were in during school. Also write down WHY you remember each of them. See if when you answer the WHY questions if they make you think of additional names.
- Draw a family tree from memory and test yourself on how far back you can go without assistance or research.
- Read a poem or a short story and then challenge yourself to summarize the main idea in 50 words or less. Now try 25. How about 10?
- Find random names in a phone book or online phone listing. Take the name and try to draw pictures of how the name sounds in order to remember the name. Do this with 5 to 10 names. Shuffle the pictures when you are finished and look at each one randomly, seeing how many pictures remind you of the correct name. If you need another association, try making up a story for each picture that memorably relates to the name.

Memory Games For Family And Friends

- Memory games with decks of cards: Lay all the cards in the deck face down in 4 equal rows of 13. Take turns choosing 2 cards and placing the face up. If they are the same rank and color they are a pair and the player wins them. If they are not a pair, they are placed face down again in their original positions. Play until all matches are made. Player with most matches wins game. Make this game more challenging by playing with 2 decks and changing rules so pairs of cards have to be identical and/or changing the layout to a circular, triangular or diamond shape, or simply lay the cards down in a random pattern.

- Place random items on a tray. Let everyone look for 30 seconds to a minute. Cover tray or take it away and have players list every item they can remember on a piece of paper. Winner is person with most correct items. Make this game more challenging by removing items and seeing who can guess what items are missing.
- Gather a hand full of coins, a handkerchief and a timer. Choose 5 coins from the pile and stack them in some sort of order. Give players short amount of time to look, then cover coins. Players then reconstruct the arrangement of coins from memory, using coins from the hand full. Winner is person who matches the original stack of coins.

Make this more challenging by adding more coins and giving players less time to study arrangement.
- Divide into two teams. One team leaves room. The other team makes 10 changes to the room. The other team then re-enters the room and tries to figure out all of the changes. Then teams switch places and repeat the process. Winning team is the one with the most correct room changes.

By Basil Foster

Brain Workouts

You may have begun this chapter by thinking, "what's the difference between brain games and brain workouts?" Are there really actual exercises that you can do that will preserve and enhance memory mind function? Not only are brain workouts a very different thing than brain games (just like there's a very big difference between playing sports and working out!), but there is an entire science devoted to brain exercise called Neurobics. The name Neurobics was created by Lawrence Katz, Ph.D. and Manning Rubin in their book *Keep Your Brain Alive* to identify these special workouts of the mind that help the brain stay in peak condition.

The main theory behind Neurobics is that the body and mind need to be moved and stimulated in unique and new ways to challenge, preserve and enhance brain and memory function, as well as combat the natural degrading effects of aging. Performing daily physical tasks with the non-dominant hand or enhancing or repressing one of the 5 senses, challenges our brains and memories to accept old activities done in new ways, this creating new associations to be consolidated, encoded and retained in the memory until it needs to be easily retrieved. Neurobics basically creates new paths in our brains that inspire our memories to accept new information as well as new associations that connect to old behaviors. If you review the sentence I just wrote it may very well remind you of descriptions of how the mind needs to be retrained to break bad habits. There is a very good reason for this, because retraining the brain and memory to accept and retain new ways to do old things is exactly the same as breaking a bad habit. Let's go back to the litany of complaints people have about their short-term memory challenges: I can't find my keys! No matter what I do, I can't keep track of my reading glasses—I must have bought 10 pairs but can I find one? Why can't I remember the name of that new woman who works in HR? I'm so tired of pretending I know my son's first grade teacher's name!

Don't all those questions and declarations sound an awful lot like bad habits? I rest my case...

Here are some Neurobic style exercises for you to try out:

- Eat breakfast using your non dominant hand for utensils
- Try washing dishes (no sharp knives!) with your eyes closed
- When you find yourself waiting in a line, balance on one foot.
- Go outside and spend some time crushing various leaves and flowers in your hands and smelling them.
- Eat spices you aren't accustomed to and think about how they taste.
- Sit on a beach, close your eyes, and sift through handfuls of sand, feeling the tiny

- stones, bits of shells, pieces of seaweed, etc.
- Instead of commercial air fresheners or room sprays, try introducing essential oils into your home.
- Brush your hair with your non dominant hand.
- Go to a local garden or nursery and look at all the different colors.
- Learn to play a musical instrument
- Try wearing yoga socks so your toes are separate and can feel the difference when you walk around.
- Go to a park and draw what you see instead of thinking about it in words
- Try to recite a poem or sing a song you know with your eyes closed.
- Try global cuisine or a new flavor of tea you've never experienced.
- Try your hand at calligraphy
- Time your daily chores and see if you can beat your best time! Give yourself a set amount of time to complete a task and see if you can beat it.
- Try out meditation or mindfulness exercises.
- Watch a comedy special or a funny TV show or movie and laugh!

- Try working to different kinds of music like classical or jazz and see how each of them makes you feel.
- Rearrange your living room furniture
- Go on a trip somewhere you've never been before.
- Try and communicate with someone who doesn't speak your language.
- Try taking alternate routes when you do errands in the car. Come back home a different way than you went. If you have the time, purposely take a detour and find your way back following landmarks or asking for directions rather than relying on your GPS.
- Change where you normally sit at home when you watch TV or eat dinner.
- Count the change in your pocket without looking at it.

The common goal of all the exercises listed above is to break out of your comfort zone and open yourself up to new experiences as well as new ways of doing old things. Getting out of any old rut in life is never a bad thing and low commitment, high experiential activities like these make change less daunting and more fun. When it comes to memory training, these types of activities all invite, in a light-hearted but memorable way, the memory to form new, vibrant associations, accessing information in unique ways that may resonate with our individual wants and needs in a deeply profound way. I also like to think that practicing Neurobics gives us tacit permission to explore and experience what life has to offer in a way we haven't allowed ourselves to since the innocence of childhood. What a gift that is!

Take Up A Memory Boosting Activity

One of the most worthwhile and comprehensive memory workouts you can give yourself is the experience of learning how to do something new. Here is a diverse list of possible learning experiences you could immerse yourself and youryour mind/memory in. Hopefully these suggestions will jumpstart your own desires to cross something off your bucket list:

Ball room or swing dancing; learning how to do magic tricks; play the cello or the banjo; French cooking lessons; botanical art classes; learning how to make furniture; organic gardening; making cheese; growing orchids; learning how to fly; coaching children's sports; playing poker; doing standup comedy; sailing; becoming a reiki master; making topiaries; building a stone wall…

Here are the benefits of embarking on any of these adventures or, for that matter any adventure of your choosing:

- **You, and your memory, learn something new:** Don't cheat yourself and pursue an activity you are already familiar

with. Your memory mind needs to be stretched in order to be flexible.
- **You get to experience a challenge:** Learning a new skill demands your undivided attention. This means your mind memory will be forced to focus. Don't give up because it's hard or feels awkward when you start learning how to do it. That's how it's supposed to feel. If it feels comfortable, you're not doing the right new activity!
- **You learn a skill that you can build upon:** Choose an activity that starts out on a basic level, but allows you to gain proficiency and that continually pushes your intellectual envelope. Choose a skill that requires you to be a lifelong learner.
- **It's gratifying:** Choose a new experience that rewards you by capturing your interest and engaging you. Don't stick with something just because it's difficult. Find a challenge you can learn to love!

Develop A Memory Exercise Routine

I have chosen the following memory boosting exercises to give you even more choices when developing your own mind memory workout schedule. Try and do at least one or two exercises a day. I promise you won't break a sweat and your engaged memory will thank you in ways

you won't believe.
- Even though we live in the wonderful world of smartphones, go old school and memorize the phone numbers of everyone in your family. Then branch out to friends and frequently dialed numbers. Who knows? You might end up saving the day during a power outage!
- Challenge yourself at the grocery store and keep a mental running tab of what you've spent while you are shopping. Amuse the cashier when you fist bump the air because your estimate came in within $5.00 of the total bill.
- Board games are all the rage again and there are some really elaborate and complicated ones on the market right now. Start a board game night and learn about new worlds and realms! This isn't your Father's scrabble game!
- Commit all those "Top 10" lists on TV, in magazines and on social media to heart. Memorize one a week or one a day.
- Memorize the lyrics to your favorite songs. You can download them for free and you will impress everyone at the next karaoke event!
- Start your own book club. Keep a book journal and write down the summary and main points of every book you read.

- Pick up a household object and come up with as many alternative uses for it as you can. Ex: a flashlight. Alternative uses: an illuminated rolling pin; an outdoor moth detector; the most important part of your lightening bug costume; a light saber for fairies; a light up baton for conducting moonlit outdoor orchestras.
- Before you fall asleep at night, mentally review the events of the day. Try to include small details. If you do this daily you will notice a definite improvement in your self-reporting skills.

Waging The War Against Distraction

Two of the greatest foes of a healthy working memory are multitasking and distraction. Unfortunately, most of us are living in a frenetically paced, internet and social media dependent society that demands we multi-task so that we can continuously sop up with our focus-fractured spongey brains, the endless detritus that results in us being so distractible. For the sake of our poor memories I've added this section, in an attempt to temporarily quiet the technical storm that has become the permanent sound-and "mind" track of our lives. So, whenever you are mindfully working on memory training, please heed the following precautions:

- Unplug: Make a hard and fast rule that when you are practicing memory improvement that does not specifically require the use of a computer, to unplug all cell phones, tablets, kindles, laptops and computers.

- Make a "Future Distractions" wish list: If you do need the services of the internet, when you are practicing your memory training, every time you are tempted to go off on an internet tangent, i.e., check your Facebook, look up a recipe, check how many times Jonny Depp has been married, or find out the current temperature in Aruba, keep paper and pen at your side to quickly jot down these distractions and diversions for another time. This will allow you to focus entirely on your memory practice and I can pretty much guarantee that a review of your distraction desires at a later date will prove both amusing and baffling
- Re-learn how to read material for comprehension, instead of skipping around from article to article like posts on a social media platform. Research has been conducted by Slate and an analytical company, Chartbeat that found that even though the reading of e-content has gone up almost 40% generally, only 5% of readers who start reading an online article actually finish it! If you have

difficulty reading efficiently for comprehension, I again urge you to pick up a copy of my book, **Speed Reading: A Practical Guide With Exercises**.
- If you are honestly having a difficult time concentrating on your memory practice, I have included two concentration exercises extracted from a definitely unplugged source: these exercises are from *The Power of Concentration*, written in 1918 by Theron Q. Dumont!
    - **Sitting Still in a Chair:** Sit in a comfortable chair and see how still you can keep. You will have to center your attention on sitting still. Never strain to keep yourself still. You must be relaxed completely. You will find this habit of relaxing is very good.
    - **Concentration on the Within:** Lie down and thoroughly relax your muscles. Concentrate on the beating of your heart. Do not pay any attention to anything else. After a little practice you can actually feel the blood passing through your system.

When I read through these rules of concentration from a century ago, I am struck by how contemporary these words of advice sound. They could have been easily written by an instructor of grounding techniques or mindfulness training. It just goes to show that everything old is new again. The art of concentration is and always has been an integral element for successful memory training. Please take the time to concentrate on your mind memory needs so that they can, in turn, serve you well throughout your life.

I would be remiss if I ended this chapter without mentioning that there is a huge amount of multi-media material on Memory training available on the Internet. As you have chosen to read about Memory Training with the purchase of this book, I have chosen to concentrate on training that can be done without the aid of a computer or the Internet; but the subject of Memory training is richly represented there as well.

The Health And Wellness Components Of Memory Training

As I did my research for this book, I kept coming across health and wellness tips interspersed among the memory tips, boosters, mnemonics, teasers, tricks, routines, and neubonics. It soon became abundantly clear that I couldn't complete this book without a chapter devoted to memory training health and wellness. And when you think about it, how could I ever have imagined it any other way? Just as memory itself cannot thrive in a vacuum, so too goes memory training, which cannot succeed without a nutritionally sound, wellness oriented support system.

Here, after much consideration and consolidation, are my top picks for memory supporting health and wellness:

Resist the temptations that add extra weight... Swedish researchers found that when overweight people lost weight, their memory and mind grew sharper. Previous research had shown that overweight people had a more difficult time recalling episodic memories, such as their first day of school, or learning how to ride a bike, but that this memory process could be improved with weight loss. It appears that the decreased ability to retrieve episodic memories was connected to insulin resistance, which can be effected by obesity. As insulin sensitivity is modulated by diet and lifestyle choices, positive changes such as balanced diet and weight loss will improve it and subsequently, brain function. Additional research demonstrated that weight loss actually changes how the brain functions. The women who participated in the trial were asked to memorize a series of names and faces and then later asked to remember the first letter of each person's name during while they had a functional MRI. The women lost an average of 17.6 pounds and improved their scores on memory test. There were also changes in brain activity. When encoding data the women's brains were more active than before they lost the weight, but when they retrieved the encoded data, their brains were less active, suggesting that weight loss made their brains more efficient. Their brains were activated and energized when learning new information but required less energy and effort when they needed to retrieve the information.

Eat a well-balanced diet that is full of memory boosting foods...
It's a well-known fact that healthy, unprocessed food in moderation is good medicine for the body. What you might not know is that there are specific foods that support healthy mind memory function. Here are the top 15 brain foods!

- Avocados – High levels of vitamin K and folate help prevent blood clots in the brain and help improve cognitive function, especially memory and concentration.

- Beets – Natural nitrates found in beets boost blood flow to the brain, helping mental performance.
- Blueberries – High levels of Gallic acid in blueberries help protect brains from degeneration and stress.
- Broccoli – The vitamin K and choline in broccoli help keep memory sharp.
- Celery – Is high in antioxidants and polysaccharides that help alleviate symptoms related to inflammation.
- Coconut Oil – Is also an anti-inflammatory and can help with memory loss as you age.
- Chocolate (dark!) – Contains flavonols which can help lower blood pressure and improve blood flow to the brain.
- Egg yolks – Are full of choline, which helps in fetal brain development.
- Extra Virgin Olive Oil – Polyphenols may not only improve learning and memory but also reverse age and disease related changes.
- Green Leafy Vegetables – Can help prevent dementia.
- Rosemary – Contains carnosic acid, helps protect the brain from neurodegeneration.
- Salmon – Is full of omega-3 fatty acids, to help your brain run smoothly and improve memory.

- Turmeric – Helps boost antioxidant levels and improves your brain's oxygen intake, keeping you alert and able to process information.
- Walnuts—Improve cognitive health, improve mental alertness and contains Vitamin E, which can help prevent Alzheimer's disease.

Monitor your blood levels...
There are several ways in which blood levels and conditions can affect memory function. Low and high blood sugar levels can cause both short-term and long-term damage to the memory mind. When blood sugar levels are too low, temporary word retrieval issues and confusion may occur until blood sugar levels are increased to normal range values. Poorly controlled diabetes, which results in high blood sugar levels, can eventually lead to long-term memory dysfunction when blood vessels are damaged causing cognitive problems and vascular dementia. There is also speculation that high blood sugar levels cause damage in the hippocampus, which is the part of the brain that is responsible for memory.

Changes in blood pressure can also contribute to memory function. High blood pressure can cause mild cognitive impairment and also lead to vascular dementia, as a result of narrowed and blocked arteries that supply blood to the brain. Blood pressure that is too low can also result in memory loss and confusion.

It appears that balance is always the answer, whether you are talking about blood sugar levels or blood pressure.

Having too much calcium in your blood (hypercalcemia) can also cause memory loss and having lead poisoning can cause irreversible memory damage, so the earlier it is detected in the blood, the better.

Educate yourself and become a life-long learner...

Using a chicken/egg model for memory and learning, it is safe to say that if we don't have or maintain the capacity to learn, there basically is no reason for memory. Conversely, without the associative and connective functions of memory, learning becomes meaningless; mere fact collecting that can't be made memorable is an exercise in futility. So memory and learning are a classic co-dependent duo. In other words we need to "learn to remember". When people make the life choice to keep learning new things, they prescriptively foster the elemental relationship between learning and memory, guaranteeing continued success both in their ability to master skills and abilities and to incorporate these new tools into the knowledge bank called memory.

Master depression, anxiety and stress...

Stress, depression and anxiety can all affect memory function, causing forgetfulness, confusion, apathy and concentration difficulties. Memory loss anxiety and/or stress symptoms include:

- Difficulty learning; blocking and memory retrieval issues; short-term memory challenges, resulting in the inability to find things, who you just called or what you spoke about; forgetting things that you normally remember; difficulty in learning new concepts; "holes" or gaps in your memory; distractibility; "brain fog"; and an inability to focus.

Memory loss depression symptoms include:
- Word retrieval issues; forgetting recent conversations; working memory issues such as the inability to hold multiple items in short-term memory; losing the thread of autobiographical memory.

Stress, anxiety and depression should never be ignored or left untreated. Seek professional medical help if you feel any of these issues are taking control of your ability to function normally in your daily life. The good news is that once mental health issues have been appropriately addressed and treated, every single memory technique presented in this book will help you prevent their reoccurrence, breaking the vicious cycle of emotional and mental distress and their negative affect on the memory mind.

Be in the moment so your memory can handle the past and the future

In keeping with the main idea of the previous point, it is imperative that you maintain a conscious presence as much as possible to ensure that your mind memory is in the vest place to function optimally. In other words, you need to exist in the here and now in order for your memory to be able to do the best job it can. There are many ways to focus your attention on the present moment and to be an active, responsive participant in your own life. The following techniques and practices will all help you to "stay in the moment".

- Grounding techniques; mind-body connections; mindfulness; meditation; yoga; tai chi; guided imagery; Reiki; biofeedback; prayer; cognitive behavioral therapy; music, art and dance/movement therapies; hypnosis; Qigong; therapeutic breathing.

General self-care is also a crucial element of consistent memory health. It really is true that you are no good to anyone else until you've been good to yourself.

Exercise makes for good memories...
Physical activity positively affects the brain in many ways. It increases heart rate, which in turn pumps more oxygen to the brain. It also helps the body release lots of hormones, which contribute, to a nourishing environment for brain cell growth and development. Exercise stimulates brain plasticity, or flexibility by encouraging the

growth of new connections between cells in all sorts of important areas of the brain. Aerobic exercise can have an antidepressant effect on stress hormones and encourage cell growth in the hippocampus, which is the part of the brain that controls that dynamic duo, learning and memory. Interestingly the type of exercise you do will determine how brain and memory function are affected.

Choosing a memorable physical activity...

- Generally speaking, if it's good for your heart, it's great for your brain.
- Choose Aerobic for improved brain function as well as to repair damaged brain cells.
- Exercise in the morning to spike brain activity, prepare you for the mental stressors of the day, and increase retention of incoming information as well as improve your reactivity to complex situations.
- When choosing a new physical activity, look for one that pairs up coordination and cardio, such as a dance class.
- If you prefer gym workouts, choose circuit training, which will spike your heart rate and piqué, your interest by constantly redirecting your attention.
- Long distance walking, running, biking or swimming can lull you into a meditative

state, perfect for processing information and problem solving.

Rest is reassuring to the mind...
Thanks to numerous imaging and behavioral studies, it has been proven that sleep plays an integral role in those two perennial favorites, learning and memory, in two major ways:
- Sleep allows memory consolidation to occur, so that all the hooks and memorable associations we have made to new information throughout the previous day, have a chance to connect to our bank of knowledge, so that it will be easily retrievable when and if we need it in the future.
- Sleep deprivation robs the memory mind of the ability to focus and learn efficiently.

Sleep also affects physical reflects, which in turn affects memory access and associative functions. It can affect fine motor skills, which are used for writing and drawing, two highly memorable associative skills for memory making. Judgment is also affected, which changes people's capability to understand the consequences of their behavior, which requires access to the appropriate response to an action from long-term memory. Studies that included memory tests show that after a single night of quality shut eye or even a good nap, participants performed better on tests, in the workplace, on the playing field or in a performance capacity.

Here are some sleep tips to help you get the proper down time your memory mind requires:
- Keep consistent sleep and wake up times, even on weekends, holidays and vacations.
- Don't exercise close to bedtime. Allow at least three hours between physical activity and sleep.
- Avoid caffeine, nicotine and alcohol before sleeping.
- Transition to a resting state by bathing, reading, drinking herbal tea and thinking stress free thoughts.
- Stop eating two to three hours before going to sleep.
- Make your bedroom a sleep sanctuary – dark, cool and comfy.
- Block out distracting noise with white noise, using a sound machine, fan or dehumidifier.
- Unplug from the virtual world. There's no room in your bed for cell phones, tablets, TV, Netflix or twitter!

All of this advice is terrific except for one little detail: how can you turn this valuable information into a memorable association worthy of consolidation into your long-term memory?
Well, you could try this:
Take the first word from each of these eight

tips—
- Resist
- Eat
- Monitor
- Educate
- Make
- Be
- Exercise
- Rest

These are all action words that should help you associate their specific health and wellness suggestions. But it gets better! Take the first letter of each of these words:
R.E.M.E.M.B.E.R.
What do you think of that? Hopefully this mnemonic will resonate with you, but if it doesn't have no fear. That's the beauty of memory training – look through all of the techniques we've explored in this book and choose one that speaks to you and your memory, or use one as a launching pad to create your own memory training techniques. I challenge you to find your own memorable way to encode and consolidate this information, as well as all the information you are now so much better prepared to discover. Good luck and here's to happy and healthy memories!

Memory Training Outcomes

If you have read this book from beginning to end here are the chronological outcomes you should have experienced and learned about:
- Common memory challenges
- Ascertaining personal memory challenges, i.e., Procedural Long-term Memory, Declarative Long-term Memory and/or Short-term Memory
- The definition of Procedural Long-term Memory
- The benefits of Mental Rehearsal
- How to Mentally Rehearse
- Why Movement aids Procedural Memory acquisition
- What Kinesthetic Learning is
- How to cue Procedural Memory with gestures and objects
- How to avoid and repair "Action Slips"
- The definition of Declarative (Semantic) Long-term Memory
- The difference between Cognitively Passive and Cognitively Active study behaviors
- Cognitively Active Study Technique Best Practices
- Learning exercises that access and utilize Semantic Memory
- The Steps of Elaborative Rehearsal

- Semantic Priming
- Using Retrieval Codes
- Using the SQ3R method of study
- Creating and implementing Semantic Scripts
- The definition of Declarative (Episodic) Long-term Memory
- How to learn and remember new names
- How to remember where you left things
- How to remember what people tell you
- How to remember to do things
- The steps of the Loci technique
- The definition of Short-term and/or Working Memory
- How Chunking works
- The definition of Photographic Memory
- The steps of The Memory Palace
- The steps of Memory Pegging
- The steps of The Military Method
- How to develop Photographic Memory with a deck of cards
- What Patterned Study Arrangements are
- How to use the Visualization and Association technique
- How to use Mind Mapping
- What Mnemonics are
- How to use Body Part Mnemonics
- How to use Musical Mnemonics
- How to use Name Mnemonics

- How to use Expression or Word Mnemonics
- How to use Model Mnemonics
- How to use Ode Mnemonics
- How to Use Note Organization Mnemonics
- How to use Connection Mnemonics
- How to use Spelling Mnemonics
- What Brain Games are
- Brain Games for Short-term and Working
- Brain Games for Long-term Memory
- Memory Games for Family and Friends
- What Brain Workouts are
- What Neurobics are
- Neurobic Style Exercises
- How to take up a Memory Boosting Activity
- Developing a Memory Exercise Routine
- How to Eliminate Distractions
- Why health and wellness matters in Memory Training
- The eight steps of memory health and wellness

Just as a maximum-efficiency memory mind allows you to leap from learning-to-read to reading-to-learn, so I hope that you will be able to make the leap from learning about memory's infinite power and potential to a consistent routine of memory training best practices. In so doing, you will gain the proficiency and confidence required to think outside of the box and to invent your own memory training techniques.

As I conducted my research and wrote this compendium of all things memory, I was struck again and again by the extraordinary ability of people to find beautifully crafted and elegantly simple solutions to the complex and abstract challenges of the human mind and memory. I am also blown away by the creativity and unique, yet universal, truths of some of these memory techniques. The ability to capture a memory lesson through a line drawing, two lines of rhyming verse or using the human body as a canvas for memory pegging is awe-inspiring. The fact that these very individual perspectives also have the ability to communicate a concept with a universal audience who will implement and use these methods for hundreds of years catapults what started as simply "a way to remember" into the realms of folk tales, universal truths and Greek mythology. What a literally unforgettable legacy we have been given, much like the miraculous gift of each of our memory minds. Perhaps you, too, will devise a memory training device that will solve a universal memory dilemma, and will be adopted and utilized by human beings around the world for the foreseeable future. The only things you need to accomplish such an incredible task are a memory challenge, the need to solve it, and the unique perspective that only your special mind and memory can conjure up. How ironic yet wonderful is it to realize that the genius who wrote "30 days has September..." must have had a problem remembering how many days were in each month of the year? I wish you well in your memory training endeavors and look forward to the day I might potentially stumble across your solution to my own memory challenges.

Memory Training

By Basil Foster

You may also like…
SPEED READING
HOW TO READ FAST FASTER
BY BASIL FOSTER

Ground breaking speed reading guide with scientifically proven benefits....

Are you tired of reading at a snail's pace? Are you fed up with not being able to remember the information that you read? Would you like to be able to improve your ability to concentrate? If you have answered yes to any of these questions, you have come to the right place!

By Basil Foster

FREE DOWNLOAD

INSIGHTFUL GROWTH STRATEGIES FOR YOUR PERSONAL AND PROFESSIONAL SUCCESS!

My friends and colleagues Joshua Moore and Helen Glasgow provided their best seller on personal and professional growth strategies as a gift for my readers.
Sign up here to get a free copy of the Growth Mindset book and more:
www.frenchnumber.net/growth

You may also like...
EMOTIONAL INTELLIGENCE SPECTRUM
EXPLORE YOUR EMOTIONS AND IMPROVE YOUR
INTRAPERSONAL INTELLIGENCE
BY JOSHUA MOORE AND HELEN GLASGOW

Emotional Intelligence Spectrum is the one book you need to buy if you've been curious about Emotional Intelligence, how it affects you personally, how to interpret EI in others and how to utilize Emotional Quotient in every aspect of your life.

Once you understand how EQ works, by taking a simple test, which is included in this guide, you will learn to harness the power of Emotional Intelligence and use it to further your career as you learn how to connect with people better.

You may also like...
I AM AN EMPATH
ENERGY HEALING GUIDE FOR EMPATHIC AND HIGHLY SENSITIVE PEOPLE
BY JOSHUA MOORE

Am an Empath is an empathy guide on managing emotional anxiety, coping with being over emotional and using intuition to benefit from this sensitivity in your everyday life – the problems highly sensitive people normally face.

Through recongnizing how to control emotions you have the potential to make the most of being in tune with your emotions and understanding the feelings of people around you.
Begin your journey to a fulfilling life of awareness and support today!

You may also like...
MAKE ROOM FOR MINIMALISM
A PRACTICAL GUIDE TO SIMPLE AND SUSTAINABLE LIVING
BY JOSHUA MOORE

By Basil Foster

Make Room for Minimalism is a clear cut yet powerful, step-by-step introduction to minimalism, a sustainable lifestyle that will enable you to finally clear away all the physical, mental and spiritual clutter that fills many of our current stress filled lives. Minimalism will help you redefine what is truly meaningful in your life.

Eager to experience the world of minimalism?
Add a single copy of **Make Room for Minimalism** to your library now, and start counting the books you will no longer need!

FNº

Presented by French Number Publishing
French Number Publishing is an independent
publishing house headquartered in Paris, France
with offices in North America, Europe, and Asia.
FNº is committed to connect the most promising
writers to readers from all around the world.
Together we aim to explore the most challenging
issues on a large variety of topics that are of
interest to the modern society.

FNº

Made in the USA
Middletown, DE
17 April 2018